AAHARAM
Sadhya

SHOBHA PILLAI COUTINHO

"

Dedicated to Amma
who did not let me cook
yet inspired me
to cook.

"

Introduction

The home cooking up a sadhya resonates with a special energy. It exudes a magical joy that gets infused into the spirit of the chef as well as her numerous assistants. They say the emotions experienced while cooking transcend into the food cooked which is why eaters of the sadhya leave their banana leaves totally satiated.

So what is a sadhya? Sadhya is a traditional banquet of Kerala. Though most of the items in a sadhya are everyday eats, when it comes together with the rest of the items, it undergoes a divine change. It is a vegetarian's delight. A mindboggling variety of vegetables are cooked in an age-old way; nothing changes from the way it was intended to be. No takers for molecular fusion here. It's made the way ammumma (grandmother) made it the way hers did. Sadhya is always served on festive occasions on a banana leaf. It is said that the health benefits of the sadhya increase when served hot on a banana leaf, as it takes in the health properties of the leaf as well. And the right way to enjoy a sadhya is with your hands, eating a sadhya with a fork and spoon is blasphemous.

The author of this recipe book, Shobha (Backwaters Chechie), has lived her dream through this book. Her experiences of hanging around in the ancestral home of her grandparents have been pasted on to the pages of the book, replete with smells, tastes and sounds. All the recipes are just the way her ammumma made it. Shobha's attempts to cook were always thwarted by an indulgent mother, maybe because ten is no age to cook, but then feisty Shobha wouldn't give up. She would sneak into the kitchen when she was sure her mother wasn't expected to be in her domain and cook up a storm literally, only to remove all traces of it before anyone could get a whiff of what had transpired. Her partners in this crime were her four sisters, they enjoyed everything she whipped up and would encourage her to do more.

For Shobha, her ammumma's kitchen in Mavelikara, Vazhuvadiyil Veedu, Vettiyar, was the stuff her dreams were made of. A cauldron of boiling curry, colourful mountains of vegetables, the tantalising aroma of spice hanging in the air, the sounds of the coconut cracking under the aruval (heavy, curved iron knife), the aroma of spices blending with coconut oil...it left an indelible mark on her young mind. It became her favourite place during her numerous summer holiday visits. It was here that the seeds of a lifelong passion took root. And it is this tapestry of experiences that has made its way into the pages of this recipe book.

So ladies and gentlemen, presenting to you Aaharam, a coming together of food items that is guaranteed to take you to gastronomical heaven that only the brave will attempt to partake on a working day! It is sure to induce a food coma that calls for at least an hour or two of sinking into a delicious stupor. Every recipe of every item in this sadhya is what she heard from her ammumma, her effort of recreating it painstakingly is the stuff great sadhyas are made of. The book is packed with recipes that are written in a simple, easy-to-follow format. Try it out and do reach out to our Shobha with your honest feedback, because she has laid it all out for you with a heart full of love. (Email: backwaterschechie@gmail.com, WhatsApp: 9820506506, 9004283333) And most importantly, it is blessed by her Ammumma and Amma.

Sugatha Menon
Communication consultant

Vote of thanks

I would like to express my sincere gratitude to all those who have helped me fulfil my fondest dream of publishing a recipe book. It would have remained a dream if it wasn't for the immense love and support that I have received along the way.

A quality book needs a quality editor and Sugatha Menon is brilliant at what she does. Thank you Sugatha for helping me convert my heartfelt emotions into words. For helping me in expressing myself and my message in the best possible manner. I would love to take the opportunity to thank one of the most creative heads that I've come across in an eventful career spanning over two decades, my Creative Director, Radhika Tipnis. This project reflects your direction and you helped this book immensely with your creative zest.

I want to thank our copy editor Rama Ramanan for dotting the 'i's, crossing the 't's, and ensuring the written word in the book is in good health. I also express my sincere gratitude and appreciation for the efforts of my talented photographer Vikas Swades Sharma. A visual is worth a thousand words and you have helped me paint a marvellous picture by bringing my food to life.

Talking of bringing food to life, I'd like to thank my food stylist, Nikita Rao, for making the sadhya look equally appetising and sumptuous for my readers. Geechi, Suma, Beena, Parvati, Greta, Rita, Tressy and Trevin, thank you for being my support system. You'll were the spark I needed and lit the fire in me that burned bright enough for me to conquer my Everest. Lots of love and blessings.

I can't thank Sonali, my domestic support, enough for all the running around and support extended. Lastly, I'd like to express sincere gratitude towards my husband Lancy and children Joshua and Jadyn, who have been my greatest support and my backbone. Your immense love and support have made this book what I wanted it to be — a reflection of my genuine passion and affection for the art of cooking.

Lots of love to my readers. Wishing you a good read, some happy meals, and great food adventures and experiences.

Cheers!
Shobha Pillai Coutinho

Foreword

Food is more than just nourishment. It is a source of joy and envy. Culinary pursuits can be need-driven, aspirational, or simply recreational. Fragrances ignite memories as food does emotions; passion for food often knows no boundaries. Cultures and rituals have been built around food; it is an integral part of rituals and ceremonies. That's why there can never be enough cookbooks and shows.

The word 'Sadhya' sparks instant smiles in South Indians, bringing fond memories of family gatherings in wet weather, feasts served on freshly cut moist banana leaves adding their own flavour to the magical food served. Foods of Kerala are rich in spices, laced with coconut, delicious, and good for health. The proportion of protein to carbohydrates (lentils to rice) in dosas is what the US FDA recommends as an ideal protein to carbs mix for a balanced diet. Most Master Chefs, I've interacted with, endeavour to make food as authentic as possible; they go to great lengths to do this and rightly so, authenticity is vital. Which in turn means preparing each dish like a local would have the same local spices and raw materials. Backwaters Chechie aka Shobha

Pillai Coutinho is as authentic as one can get. Born and raised a Malayalee, she has a lifetime of experience with Kerala cuisine, and her pedigree is perfect for the book. A young, multi-talented Shobha started her career over thirty years ago with India's leading media house. Three decades later, she is still with them and has risen to the top as an integral part of the core team, a senior pillar of the organization. Her stable career graph is accompanied by an equally envious personal life. Shobha lives in Mumbai, married to the love of her life who has also been working in the same organisation for a similar duration. Their lives are complemented by their two very humble, well-cultured sons, both budding young stars.

On a trip to India after a four-year gap overseas, I found myself at a mini Sadhya prepped by Shobha. Few words can convey the explosion of tastes, fragrances and memories that occurred with every fresh bite into the Kerala delicacies by Backwaters Chechie.

Shobha's culinary skills put down into this book ensure a perfect legacy for our best culinary traditions. I'm sure you will enjoy and use this book as much as I do.

Best Wishes,
Captain Vinod Nair

(Author, Coach, Business Consultant, Investor)

Backwaters Chechie ™

By God it's Authentic!

Aharam ~ Sadhya
Author: Shobha Pillai Coutinho
Copyrights: Shobha Pillai Coutinho
Editor: Sugatha Menon
Copy Editor: Rama Ramanan
Visual Concept Design, Typography: Radhika Tipnis
Photography: Vikas Swades Sharma
Food Styling, Art Direction: Nikita Rao

Publisher:

Shobha Pillai Coutinho
Evershine Millenium Paradise,
EMP Tower, 47/203, Halley building Phase 5,
Thakur village, Kandivili East
Mumbai 400101

First Edition: 2022

ISBN: 978-93-5701-729-9

Price: INR 1199/-

Contents

Kadugu Maanga

(Mango Pickle)

—

Raw mango pickle is a high source of vitamin C and antioxidants.

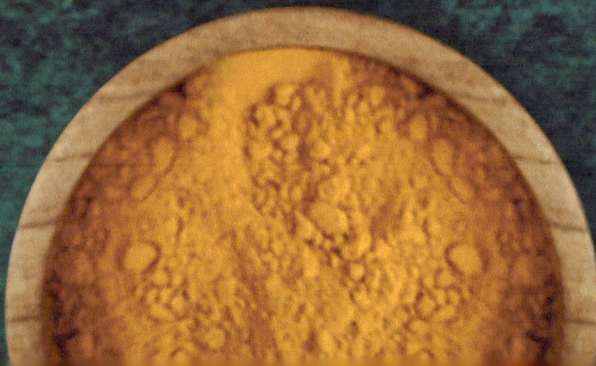

Preparation time: 30 minutes

Ingredients

Raw mango: 1 kg

Red chilli powder: 1 tbsp

Kashmiri chilli powder: 3 tbsp

Roasted fenugreek powder: 1 tsp

Turmeric powder: 1 tsp

Whole red chillies: 4

Asafoetida: 1 tsp

Curry leaves: 3 to 4 sprigs

A dash of fenugreek powder

Sesame oil for seasoning: 2 to 3 tbsp

Preparation

Wash and cut the raw mangoes into small pieces. Add red chillies powder, fenugreek powder, turmeric powder, asafoetida and salt. Give it a good mix upside down and keep it aside. You may add ½ a cup of boiled and cooled water to increase the consistency.

Seasoning

- Heat oil in a heavy-bottom pan and add mustard seeds. Once it splutters, add red chillies, curry leaves, fenugreek powder, chilli powder, and asafoetida. Mix well and switch off the flame.

- Add this mixture to the marinated mango pieces and mix it well. Close it with a lid. After half an hour, you may fill this in aachaar bharani.

Tips

Use roasted fenugreek powder.

You may sprinkle a dash of mustard powder (optional).

Add 1 teaspoon of chopped ginger and garlic (optional) while marinating.

....

Health benefits

Pickle is said to generate endorphins (happy hormones) and aid digestion.

Naranga Curry

The tangy, spicy lemon pickle spices up the rest of the sadhya.

Preparation time: 30 minutes

Ingredients

Wild lemon: ½ kg

Chilli powder: 2 tbsp
(Kashmiri chilli powder)

Turmeric powder: ¼ tsp

Asafoetida powder: 1 tsp

Fenugreek powder: ¼ tsp, roasted

Turmeric powder: a pinch

Mustard seeds: 1 tsp

Sesame oil: 2 tbsp

Dry red chillies: 2 to 3

Green chillies: 3

Ginger: 2 inch piece, chopped

Curry leaves: 2 sprigs

Salt to taste

Water: ½ cup
(boiled and cooled water)

Jaggery (optional): ¼ tsp

Preparation

Cut the lemon into small pieces after removing the seeds. Add chopped ginger, green chillies cut in a round shape, chopped curry leaves, salt, and turmeric powder. Add 2 tablespoons of water, mix it well and keep it aside for half an hour.

Seasoning

- In a frying pan, add oil. Once it's hot, add mustard seeds followed by red chillies and curry leaves. Switch off the flame.

- Add red chilli powder, roasted fenugreek powder, asafoetida powder, and give it a good mix. Garnish the above lemon mixture. You may add ¼ teaspoon jaggery to balance the level of salt and spice.

- Naranga curry is ready to serve.

Tips

To reduce the bitter taste, remove the seeds and inner white layers. But do not remove the skin as this will spoil the texture of the pickle.

....

Health benefits

Lemons are the richest source of vitamin C.

Inji Puli or Inji Curry

(Ginger tamarind chutney)

A delightful combination of sweet and sour with a refreshing burst of ginger. Inji puli is a must-have in sadhyas.

Preparation time: 30 minutes

Serves: 15-20 people

Ingredients

Fresh ginger: 250 g, skin to be peeled and cut into a thin round shape, or chopped finely

Shallots (small onions): 10 to 15, cut in thin and round shape

Green chillies: 4 to 5, cut in round shape (you can add more depending on your spice preference. Keep in mind that ginger also adds to the spice naturally.)

Tamarind: 50 g (approx.) or 1 big lemon size ball. Soak the tamarind in one cup of hot water. Squeeze the tamarind well, strain the water and keep it aside.

Curry leaves: 2 to 3 sprigs (pick the ones with good aroma and flavour)

Jaggery: 6 to 8 tsp

Salt to taste

Spices

Chilli powder: 2 tbsp

Turmeric powder: ½ tbsp

Coriander powder: ½ tbsp

Asafoetida (optional): ¼ tbsp

Fenugreek powder: ¼ tsp, roasted and powdered

Seasoning

Coconut oil/sesame oil: 4 to 5 tbsp

Curry leaves: 1 sprig

Red dry chillies: 1 sprig

Mustard seeds: 1½ tsp

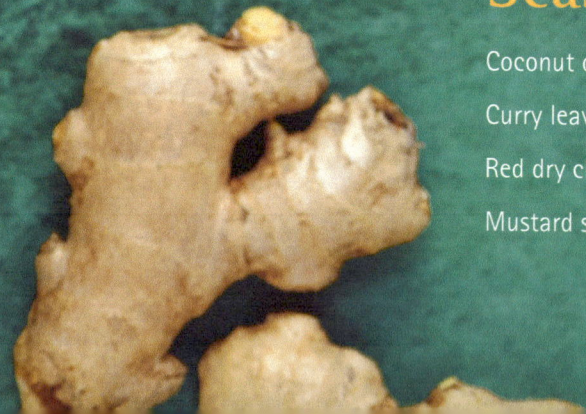

Preparation

- Heat a frying pan and add 2 to 3 tablespoons of coconut oil to it. Add the ginger and sauté for two minutes till it turns golden brown and crispy. Then, keep it aside to cool.

- In the same oil, on a low flame, add shallots and curry leaves. Sauté till shallots are almost golden brown, and then add this mixture to' the ginger. Allow it to cool.

- Once this mixture is cool, grind it to a crumb-like consistency, but not very thin powder. It should be slightly crushed, just enough to get small crumbs of ginger while eating.

- In the same hot oil, add green chillies and curry leaves; fry them on a low flame. This is the perfect time to add spices.

- Add turmeric powder and sauté it well. Add coriander powder and mix it properly until the raw smell goes away. Remember, all spices must be added on low flame only.

- Add fenugreek powder, asafoetida and chilli powder; give it a good mix.

- Now on high flame, add the tamarind water and a cup of hot water. Bring it to a boil and add salt.

- On a low flame, add the crushed ginger to this mixture and allow it to boil. Keep stirring as it gets thicker.

- This is the perfect time to add jaggery. Keep stirring till the jaggery melts in the tamarind water. Add half a cup of hot water to maintain consistency, and cook for 5 to 7 minutes.

- Turn off the flame.

Seasoning

- In a seasoning pan, on a low flame, add oil. Add some mustard seeds and allow them to splutter.

- Add a few red chillies and curry leaves. Add a pinch of fenugreek powder/ asafoetida to enhance the flavour.

- Garnish the Inji curry with this and mix it well.

- Allow the same to cool. Store in a dry container for over a month or more.

TIPS

Inji curry and inji puli, both are the same. However, the quantity of tamarind is more in inji puli.

Add jaggery only when Inji curry's consistency is thick while boiling.

Adding a dash of fenugreek/ asafoetida powder for seasoning is optional.

Keep the flame low while adding any powdered spices.

Health benefits

Tamarind, ginger and jaggery, the main ingredients of this curry along with the spices, are a great way to digest the sadhya food.

Parippu

—

Parippu or boiled lentils is served as soon as steamed rice makes an appearance on the sadhya leaf. It is paired with a spoon of ghee, a combination made in heaven!

Preparation time: 20 minutes

Serves: 5 guests

Ingredients

Split moong dal (yellow), roasted: 1 cup

Grated coconut: ½ cup

Garlic flakes: 2-3

Cumin seeds: 1 tsp

Green chillies: 2 nos.

Turmeric powder: ¼ tsp

Coconut oil/Ghee: 1 tbsp

Curry leaves: 1 sprig

Seasoning

Oil/Ghee

Curry Leaves

Preparation

- In a pan, roast the dal on a medium flame for five minutes. Keep it aside to let it cool. Then, wash it thoroughly. Add a cup of water to it and cook the same on a medium flame or 2 to 3 whistles. You may add 1 teaspoon of coconut oil and salt.

- Meanwhile, in a mixer, add coconut, garlic, cumin seeds, green chillies and turmeric powder. Add some water and grind it to a smooth paste.

- Once the dal is cooked, stir it well on a medium flame and add the coconut mixture to it. You may add more water to maintain consistency. Mix it well and continue stirring for 5 to 7 minutes. Now, add a tablespoon of ghee or coconut oil. Crush a few curry leaves and add to the dal.

- Switch off the flame. Close it with a lid for 10 minutes.

TIPS

Sadhya parippu must be thick in consistency.

You may use coconut oil or ghee.

This is served on top of rice with a spoon of hot ghee.

Did you know that?

Moong dal is considered to be best for weight watchers. The iron content in this dal makes it ideal for anaemia patients too.

Sambhar

The universally popular south Indian curry that is served in every part of the globe. Packed with the goodness of vegetables and proteins, it makes for a complete meal when paired with rice.

Preparation time: 30 minutes

Serves: 6 to 8 guests

Ingredients

½ cup tur dal

Vegetables

Pumpkin: ½ cup

Ladies finger (Okra): 6 to 8

Drumstick: 8 pieces, index finger size

Raw banana: ½ cup

Cluster beans: 10 to 12

Potatoes: 2, medium size

Small brinjal: ½ cup

Yam: ½ cup

Tomato: 1

Onion: 1, medium size

Shallots: ½ cup, (approx. 15 nos.)

Green chillies: 3 to 4

Curry leaves: 2 to 3 sprigs (pick the ones with good aroma and flavour)

Grated coconut: ½ cup

Salt to taste

Tamarind: lemon size

Water: 1 cup

Spices

Dried red chillies: 10

Coriander seeds: 1 ½ tbsp

Turmeric powder: ½ tsp

Asafoetida: ½ tsp

Salt to taste

Homemade Backwaters Chechie's sambar powder: 1 tbsp, (check the recipe at the end of the book) *

Seasoning

Coconut oil: 3 tbsp

Mustard seeds: 1 tsp

Fenugreek seeds: ¼ tsp

Dried red chillies: 3 nos.

Turmeric powder: 1 tsp

Asafoetida: ½ tsp

Curry leaves: 2 sprigs

Homemade sambhar powder*

Preparation

- Wash /clean and cut all the vegetables and keep them aside.

- Soak tamarind for 15 to 20 minutes in hot water.

- Pressure cook the soaked tur dal with one teaspoon of coconut oil and water as required.

- Roast red chillies, coriander seeds and fenugreek seeds in a non-stick pan.

- Then, add freshly grated coconut and roast the same till it turns golden brown. Now, add turmeric powder and sauté well. Add asafoetida to this and allow the mixture to cool down and then grind this mixture to a smooth paste.

- In an earthen pot, heat 2 tablespoons of coconut oil, add the shallots, curry leaves and sauté till everything gets translucent. Now, add all the cut vegetables except the ladies finger. Add turmeric powder and salt. Add 3 to 4 cups of water and give it a good mix. Cover and cook the vegetables for approximately 15 minutes. Meanwhile, sauté the ladies finger in a teaspoon of oil and keep it aside. Once the vegetables are cooked, add ladies finger.

- Now add the cooked dal and coconut masala mixture. Extract the tamarind juice and add it to this paste. Add salt to taste, a few curry leaves and close the lid. Cook on low flame for 10 minutes.

- You may add water to maintain consistency as per your requirement.

Seasoning

Heat coconut oil in a seasoning pan. Add mustard seeds and once they splutter, add fenugreek seeds, red chillies, curry leaves, 1 tablespoon of BWC sambhar masala, and garnish the cooked sambhar.

TIPS

Sambhar can be made without coconut as well.

Soak a lemon size ball of tamarind.

Roast the asafoetida chunks that are not pounded in coconut oil till they turn crisp. Keep them aside to cool down and then powder. You may use pounded asafoetida as well.

Be generous with asafoetida and curry leaves for an aromatic authentic sambhar.

You may add half teaspoon of BWC sambhar masala while cooking the vegetables.

In authentic Kerala sambhar, we do not use cumin seeds and coriander leaves. You may add as per your preference.

· ·

Did you know that?

Sambhar originated in the kitchen of Shahaji Bhonsale (1684 to 1711 CE). He was the son of Ekoji, founder of the Maratha rule of Thanjavur and Chatrapati Shivaji Maharaj's stepbrother.

Avial

One of the healthiest vegetable dishes. Seasonal vegetables blended with fresh coconut and lightly spiced, Aviyal is everyone's favourite. It's a hit with weightwatchers too.

Preparation time: 30 minutes

Serves: 6 to 8 guests

Ingredients

Raw banana: 1 cup

Yam: 1 cup

Drumstick: 8 pieces, size of index finger

Cluster beans: 10 to 12

Potatoes: 2, medium size (optional)

Carrot: 1, medium size

Ash gourd: 1 cup

Onion: 1, medium size

Shallots: 10 to 12

Green chillies: 3 to 4

Curry leaves: 2 to 3 sprigs (pick the ones with good aroma and flavour)

Coconut: 1, grated

Coconut oil: 2 to 3 tbsp

Plain curd: 4 to 5 tbsp (whisked)

Salt to taste

Spices

Cumin seeds: 1 tsp

Turmeric powder: 1 tsp

Seasoning

Coconut oil: 2 tsp

Curry leaves: 2 sprigs

Preparation

- Wash, clean and cut all the vegetables lengthwise and maintain the thickness.

- In an earthen pot, add 2 tablespoons of coconut oil and slide in all the cut vegetables along with turmeric powder, two green chillies and curry leaves.

- Steam the vegetables. Add half a cup of water. You may add salt to taste. Close it with a lid and allow the vegetables to cook.

- Grind half a coconut, green chillies, shallots and cumin seeds coarsely. Add the remaining coconut to this mixture and mix it well using your hands.

- Ensure the vegetables are semi-cooked and not sticky. Now, add the coconut mixture to the steamed vegetables, but don't stir yet. Let this mixture be on top of the vegetables. Close it with a lid for five minutes and then give it a good mix without breaking the vegetables. Keep it on low flame for 5 minutes.

- Now, add 4 to 5 tablespoons of plain curd and gently mix. Season it with some more coconut oil and fresh curry leaves.

TIPS

All the vegetables should be cut approximately 2 inches long (preferably julienne them, but keep it moderately thick).

A dash of red chilli powder is recommended if you prefer the colour of the Avial to be a bit orange-hued.

Do not add water and overcook vegetables.

You may add one tomato/mango or a small portion of tamarind as a substitute for curd.

Be generous with curry leaves, coconut and coconut oil.

The spice will be from green chillies, which you may add based on your preference.

....

Health benefits

Avial is packed with minerals, vitamins and many nutrients. Rich in fiber it is an ideal dish for weightwatchers.

Preparation time: 30 minutes

Serves: 5 to 6 guests

Ingredients

Yam: 250-300 g

Raw plantain: 2 nos.

Black chickpeas (Kadala): 150 g

Coconut: 1 no.(1/2 to grind and 1/2 for seasoning)

Jaggery: 2 tsp

Cumin seeds: 1½ tsp

Turmeric powder: ½ tsp

Black pepper: 1 tsp

Chilli powder: 1 tbsp

Green chillies: 2-3 nos.

Water: 2 cups

Salt to taste

Seasoning

Grated coconut: ½

Mustard seeds: ½ tsp

Red chillies: 4 nos.

Jaggery powder: 2 tbsp

Curry leaves: 3 sprigs

Kootu Curry

A blissful union of tubers and lentils with the soothing sharpness of pepper, the kootu curry is an important item in the sadhya.

Preparation

- Soak chickpeas overnight for 5 to 6 hours before preparation. Pressure cook the same with a pinch of salt for 3 to 4 whistles. Once cooked, drain the water and keep aside.

- Cut yam into cubes of medium thickness and put them in a bowl of water to which a pinch of salt has been added, for 10 minutes. Then drain and keep aside.

- Cut the plantain into cubes of medium thickness and keep aside. Grind half coconut, cumin seeds, green chillies and with 1 tablespoon of water to a coarse paste and keep aside.

- Now, in an earthen pot, add the yam cubes, a pinch of salt and some water, close it with a lid and allow it to cook on a medium flame for 10 minutes.

- Once the yam is semi-cooked, add the plantain cubes. Give it a good mix.

- Now add turmeric powder, chilli powder and crushed pepper. This is the right time to add the coconut gravy and mix it very well. Keep it on low flame.

- Add the cooked and drained black chickpeas to the yam and plantain mixture. Give it a good mix with a wooden spatula. Add salt to taste only.

- Continue cooking till the raw coconut smell subsides. Meanwhile, add 1 or 2 tablespoons of jaggery powder to the chickpeas mixture and give it a good mix.

- Seasoning is the most important step for the aromatic and delicious Kootu curry in the making.

- Heat oil in a seasoning pan and add mustard seeds. Allow it to splutter. Add curry leaves and red chillies, followed by grated coconut from our seasoning ingredients list. Roast the coconut till golden brown on a low flame. Once this mixture turns golden brown, switch off the flame and pour it onto the chickpeas mixture. Give it a good mix.

- Garnish with a dash of crushed pepper and fresh curry leaves for aroma.

TIPS

Don't add too much water while cooking yam and plantain.

Jaggery is optional.

Health Benefits

Chickpeas are a must in your regular menu. They have a high fiber and protein content that keeps you feeling full and the best part is they have a relatively low calorie density.

Kootu Curry

14

AAHARAM | SADHYA

Olan

Olan is the quiet one in the sadhya ensemble. Pale and milky, it doesn't stand out in the personality department, but it is the perfect foil for the more robust curries and pickles.

Preparation time: 20 minutes

Serves: 5 to 6 guests

Ingredients

White pumpkin (ash gourd/Kumbalanga): 250 g, diced

Red cow peas (Vanpayar): 1/4 cup, cooked

* Coconut Milk: If homemade then 1 cup second-time pressed which will be semi-watery, and half cup first time pressed which will be thick. You may use readymade 200 ml coconut milk as well in absence of fresh coconut milk.

Green chillies: 3 to 4 nos.

Salt to taste

Curry leaves: 3 to 4 sprigs

Coconut oil: 2 tbsp

Water: $1^{1/2}$ cup

Seasoning

Curry leaves: 1 sprig

Preparation

- Peel the outer skin of the ash gourd. Remove the seeds and dice them into cubes or square (medium size).

- Slit the green chillies into two parts and keep the curry leaves ready.

- Soak the red cow peas overnight; next morning, drain all the water. Cook the peas with little salt and 1 cup of water and keep it aside.

- Heat coconut oil in a pan. Add curry leaves and slit green chillies. Once the chillies start crackling, add the diced ash gourd curry leaves and green chillies mixture, and give it a good stir.

- Now, add the coconut milk (if homemade then use 1 cup of the second pressed coconut milk). You may add salt to taste, give it a good mix and allow it to simmer for 10 minutes. The ash gourd must be cooked till its tender.

- Then, add the boiled and cooked peas to the above mixture and pour the first pressed coconut milk, on a low flame.

- When you pour the first pressed coconut milk, do not boil the same, it will curdle, just heat it. The gravy will thicken on its own.

- Then, crush the curry leaves on your palm and add to this mixture for the flavour to permeate, and stir well.

- Now add a tablespoon of fresh coconut oil and close it with a lid. Open after 30 minutes.

TIPS

The ash gourd can be diced, or cut into medium or long pieces.

You can use either readymade or homemade coconut milk.

To avoid curdling, do not boil the first coconut milk that is poured the second time.

There is no seasoning other than garnishing with coconut oil.

Be generous with curry leaves and green chillies.

Peas should not over power ash gourd.

You can add water to maintain consistency as per your requirement.

Sugar is optional.

Did you know that?

Olan can also be made with red pumpkin. But the health benefits of ash gourd are many. One benefit that stands out is that it is said that being rich in iron, regular consumption of ash gourd can help prevent brain disorders.

Kaalan

It is said that back in the days when refrigeration hadn't reached India, Kaalan was a dish that was preserved for months in earthern pots. The world is waking up to the benefits of fermented foods now, but its been a part of our cusine for eons.

Preparation time: 20 minutes

Serves: 4 to 6 guests

Ingredients

Yam: 100 g

Raw banana: 100 g

Green chillies: 4 nos.

Ghee: 1 tbsp

Curd: 1 kg, not too sour

Coconut: Half

Coconut oil: 2 tbsp

Salt to taste

Spices

Turmeric powder: ¼ tsp

Crushed pepper: ½ tsp

Cumin seeds: ¼ tsp

Fenugreek seeds: 1 tsp, roasted and powdered

Seasoning

Mustard seeds: ½ tsp

Red chillies: 3 to 4

Curry leaves: 2 sprigs

Coconut Oil

Preparation

- Peel the skin of raw banana and yam. Cut them into cubes or squares (medium-sized). Cover the pot with a lid and cook the vegetables on a low to medium flame with half to one cup of water, salt, crushed pepper and turmeric powder in an earthern pot till the water evaporates. Check at regular intervals if the yam is cooked well.

- Now, add a tablespoon of ghee and give it a good mix. Check if the vegetables are cooked well and tender. There should not be any water left in the vessel.

- Meanwhile, grind coconut, cumin seeds, and green chillies with ¼ cup of water to a smooth paste. Add this paste to the above and give it a good mix. Add curd to this mixture. If the gravy appears thick, add ¼ cup of water to maintain the consistency. Add salt to taste and bring this gravy to a boil.

- Once it's just about to boil, switch off the flame.

Seasoning

- In a seasoning pan, heat 2 teaspoons of coconut oil. Add mustard seeds and allow them to splutter.

- Add dry red chillies and curry leaves.

- Now, sprinkle ¼ teaspoon of roasted and powdered fenugreek. Mix it well and switch off the flame.

- Pour the seasoning mixture into the Kaalan curry. Cover and let the flavours permeate for 10 minutes.

TIPS

Please check at regular intervals if the yam is cooked well and add water accordingly if already evaporated.

While seasoning, please keep the flame on very low mode.

Do not burn the red chillies, just allow the colour change.

Be generous with curry leaves.

The curry will thicken on its own later, so you may add water accordingly.

When you add salt, keep in mind that we have already added salt whilst cooking the yam and raw banana.

Curd should not be boiled, it will curdle and not give you the desired results.

....

Did you know that?

Yam is an excellent food for women. It is said to ease symptoms of menopause. It is also known to have adequate amounts of micronutrients such as copper and vitamin C.

Mathanga Erisseri

The Erisseri is considered a mild curry. It does a great job of balancing out the spiciness of other items in the sadhya.

Preparation time: 30 minutes

Serves: 4 to 5 guests

Ingredients

Yellow pumpkin: 1 cup

Red cow peas: 1 cup (soaked 2 to 3 hours before cooking)

Coconut: 1 no. (1/2 to grind and 1/2 for seasoning)

Shallots: 4 to 5

Green chillies: 2

Cumin seeds: 1 tsp

Urad dal: 1 tsp

Dry red chillies: 3 to 4

Turmeric powder: ¼ tsp

Chilli powder: 1 tsp

Curry leaves: 1 sprig

Coconut oil: 1 tbsp

Water as required

Salt to taste

Seasoning

Mustard seeds: 1 tsp

Curry leaves: 1 sprig

Dry red chillies: 2 nos.

Urad dal: 1 tsp

Coconut oil: 2 to 3 tbsp

Shallots: 2 to 3 chopped

Preparation

- Cook red cow peas with some salt and then keep it aside.

- Cut the yellow pumpkin into medium cubes and cook the same with ½ teaspoon chilli powder and turmeric powder until they turn soft. Keep checking in between if the water has dried up. Accordingly, add some more water until the pumpkin is cooked well.

- Strain the water. Mash coarsely and keep it aside.

- Now mix the cooked pumpkin with the peas and give it a good mix, add water to maintain consistency.

- Grind the coconut for gravy along with green chillies, cumin seeds, shallots turmeric and some water. Make it a smooth paste.

- Add this gravy to the cooked pumpkin and peas mixture. Give it a good mix and allow it to boil for 10-12 minutes, and switch off the flame.

- Add salt to taste.

Seasoning

- In a seasoning pan, add some coconut oil. When the oil is hot, add some mustard seeds, urad dal, chopped shallots, red chillies and curry leaves. Add the coconut kept aside for seasoning. Roast the coconut till it turns golden brown.

- Switch off the flame. Add this mixture to the pumpkin peas gravy.

TIPS

You can cook the peas first in the cooker once half-cooked, Then, you can add the pumpkin and cook it till done.

Shallots is optional for grinding and seasoning.

....

Did you know that?

Red pumpkin is loaded with the goodness of beta carotene.

Red pumpkin is a very versatile vegetable. You can not only use it to make a sabzi or curry, but also cakes, cookies and other desserts.

Thoran

Thoran is a dry vegetable dish. It is usually lightly spiced and the cooking method is such that the vegetable retains its original flavour.

Preparation time: 20 minutes

Serves: 5 to 6 guests

Ingredients

Cabbage: ¼ kg

Freshly grated coconut: ½ cup

Turmeric powder: ¼ tsp

Green chillies: 2 to 3

Ginger: 1 small piece, grated

Shallots: 7 to 8

Salt to taste

Seasoning

Mustard seeds: ½ tsp

Urad dal: ½ tsp

Curry leaves: 1 sprig

Coconut oil: 3 tbsp

Preparation

• Chop the cabbage fine and keep it aside.

• Grind coarsely coconut, shallots, green chillies, ginger and add this to the chopped cabbage bowl. Add turmeric powder, salt, and a few curry leaves. Give it a good mix using your hands, and keep it aside.

Seasoning

• Add 2 tablespoons of oil in a seasoning pan, and once it is hot, add mustard seeds. When it splutters, add urad dal, red chillies and curry leaves.

• Now, add the cabbage mixture to this pan. Stir it well, cover this mixture with a lid and keep it on low flame for five minutes. Remove the lid, stir it well and keep it open on low flame for 2 to 3 minutes, and then switch off the flame.

TIPS

You can also add finely chopped beans and carrots to the chopped cabbage.

The coconut and the remaining ingredients mentioned should not be ground to a paste. It should be coarsely ground.

While seasoning, take utmost care to keep the flame low so that the ingredients don't burn. Add salt if needed.

Cabbages have been in cultivation for more than 4,000 years. China, India and Russia are the top three cabbage cultivators. It is a storehouse of many vital vitamins and other nutrients.

Mezhukkupuratti

—

Mezhukkupuratti is a light, healthy and perfect accompaniment to the healthy rice gruel, kanji. Usually made of raw plantains and string beans, it's a staple in many homes in Kerala.

Preparation time: 20 minutes

Serves: 6 to 8 guests

Ingredients

Raw Kerala banana: 4 to 5

Green chillies: 3 to 4, slit

Turmeric powder: ¼ tsp

Curry leaves: 3 sprigs

Salt to taste

Coconut oil: 4 to 5 tbsp

Preparation

- Wash and clean the bananas very well. Trim the edges, peel the skin and cut the same into small cubes. Dip these cubes in water for 5 to 10 minutes.

- In a pan, cook these raw bananas along with some water, salt, and turmeric powder. Cook until semi-soft, but ensure it doesn't turn mushy. Keep this aside.

- Heat oil in a frying pan, add green chillies, curry leaves, banana pieces, salt, and a dash of turmeric powder. Just toss around occasionally till well-blended and ensure it is slightly moist and not too dry.

TIPS

Coconut oil must get the flavour and authentic Mezhukkupuratti taste.

Rasam

Rasam is said to have originated in Madurai in the 16th century but it is very much a part of the daily cuisine of Kerala. A must-have in sadhyas, it is usually served towards the end with the last round of rice.

Preparation time: 20 minutes

Serves: 6 guests

Ingredients

Tur dal: 3 to 4 tbsp

Tomatoes: 4

Tamarind: 1 lemon size

Pepper: 1 tsp, crushed

Ghee/Oil: 3 tbsp

Turmeric powder: ¼ tsp

Coriander seeds: 1 tsp

Shallots: 3 to 4

Green chilies: 2 to 3 (optional)

Garlic with skin: 10 to 12 cloves

Ginger: 1 small piece

Coriander leaves: fist full

Jaggery (optional): ¼ tsp

Salt to taste

Seasoning

Mustard seeds: 1 tsp

Asafoetida: 1 tsp

Curry leaves: 2 sprigs

Fenugreek powder: ½ tsp, roasted

Red chillies: 3 nos.

Kashmiri chilli powder: 1 tsp

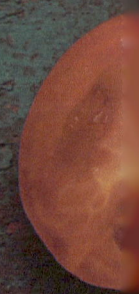

Preparation

- Cook tur dal with tomatoes, turmeric powder, one teaspoon ghee and salt. Mash it well and keep it aside. Add half of the tamarind water and three cups of hot water to this cooked dal, and bring this to a boil for 10 minutes. Add 2 to 3 curry leaves and switch off the flame.

- Now, crush pepper, ginger, green chillies, coriander seeds, garlic and shallots. Keep them aside.

Seasoning

- In a frying pan, add two tablespoons of ghee/oil. Then, add mustard seeds and allow them to splutter. Now, add the crushed ingredients to this and give it a good mix. Add red chillies, 1/4 teaspoon of fenugreek powder, curry leaves and 1/2 teaspoon of asafoetida powder. Finally, add 1 teaspoon of Kashmiri chilli powder and give it a good mix.

- Now, add the cooked dal mixture to the seasoning. Add the remaining tamarind water and salt to taste. Stir it well.

- To balance the spice and salt, you may add a teaspoon of jaggery (this is optional). Add coriander leaves; keep it on low flame and cover it with a lid and switch off the flame. Keep it aside.

TIPS

Tur dal is optional (you may use the rest of the ingredients and follow the process).

You may use ghee or coconut ghee or coconut oil.

Green chillies are optional. You may crush it along with the crushed ingredients or use it for garnishing.

You may add a pinch of asafoetida while cooking the dal.

Be generous with crushed pepper as it gives an authentic flavour to rasam.

You may add more water as per your requirement.

Rasam is an excellent remedy to combat common cold. Nothing like a fiery hot rasam to open up a blocked nose!

Pineapple Pachadi

Relatively a new entrant in the world of sadhya, it is today one of the most popular items on the leaf, especially amongst non Malayalis.

Preparation time: 20 minutes

Serves: 5 to 6 guests

Ingredients

Ripe pineapple: 500 g

Cumin seeds: ½ tsp

Crushed mustard powder: ¼ tsp

Turmeric powder: ½ tsp

Chilli powder: ½ tsp

Green chillies: 2-3

Sugar or jaggery (optional): 1 tbsp

Salt to taste

Seasoning

Coconut oil: 3 tbsp

Mustard seeds: 1 tsp

Red chillies: 2 nos.

Curry leaves: 1 sprig

Preparation

- Peel the pineapple skin. Remove the thick pieces and retain the soft ones. Dice them into cubes or squares (medium-sized).

- In a cooker, add the pineapple pieces, 2 to 3 tablespoons of water, turmeric and chilli powder, salt and a few curry leaves. Cook for approximately 3 to 4 whistles on medium flame.

- Meanwhile, grind coconut, cumin seeds, mustard seeds, green chillies, and add turmeric powder, to make a smooth paste. Add 2 tablespoons of water to this paste and keep it aside.

- Crush a small piece of pineapple to check if it's cooked well, and also monitor the sweetness. Add 1 tablespoon of jaggery powder or sugar if needed.

- Now, add the coconut mixture and cook for at least 10 minutes. Stir well and then add 2 to 3 tablespoons of curd; give it a good mix. Please do not boil this mixture after adding curd. Switch off the gas. Check for consistency of salt.

Seasoning

In a seasoning pan, pour some oil. Once it's sufficiently hot, add mustard seeds, red chillies, and curry leaves. Add this garnish to Pineapple Pachadi.

TIPS

Use ripe pineapple. If it is very sweet, then you may avoid using jaggery/sugar in the recipe.

Do not boil the gravy once the curd is added.

You may use crushed mustard or mustard seeds to grind or sprinkle crushed mustard into the coconut gravy.

Did you know that?

Did you know that India is the sixth largest producer of pineapple. It grows abundantly in North East, Kerala, Karnataka, West Bengal, Bihar, Goa and Maharashtra.

Beetroot Pachadi

On the green banana leaf, most of the items are in shades of yellow or orange; the Beetroot Pachadi with its delicious, vivi pink stands out.

Preparation time: 20 minutes

Serves: 4 to 5 guests

Ingredients

Beetroot: 2-3 medium-sized

Water: ½ cup

Grated coconut: ½ cup

Mustard: 1 tbsp (for grinding ½ tsp optional), and 1 tsp for seasoning

Cumin seeds: ½ tsp

Ginger: 1 small piece

Green chillies: 2-3 nos.

Sugar is optional (just to balance sourness/salt/sweetness)

Curd: 500 g

Seasoning

Mustard seeds: 1 tsp

Red chillies: 2 nos.

Curry leaves: 1 sprig

Coconut oil: 3 tbsp

Preparation

- Peel the beetroot. Grate the same in a grater and keep aside.

- In an earthen open pot, add the grated beetroot, 2 to 3 tablespoons of water, salt and few curry leaves, and cook for approximately 5 to 7 minutes on a medium flame. Close the pot with an appropriate lid.

- Meanwhile grind coconut, cumin seeds, mustard seeds, green chillies, ginger, to a smooth paste. You may add 2 tablespoons of water and keep this aside.

- By now the beetroot is very well cooked. Check the sweetness of the beetroot. Accordingly, you may add 1 tablespoon of jaggery Powder or sugar to maintain the sweetness (optional).

- This is the perfect time to add the coconut mixture and cook it for at least 10 minutes. Ensure the water is evaporated and the mixture is dry. You can turn off the flame now. Stir it well and add curd and give it a good mix. Please do not boil this mixture once curd is added.

- Check salt and add to taste.

Seasoning

In a seasoning pan, once the oil is hot, add some mustard seeds, red chillies, curry leaves and garnish the Beetroot Pachadi.

TIPS

Use deep, red-coloured, globe-shaped beetroot.

Ensure the beets are not limp and mushy. If very sweet, then you may avoid jaggery/sugar.

Do not boil the gravy once curd is added.

You may use mustard or mustard powder or seeds to grind or you may sprinkle crushed mustard to the coconut gravy as well.

....

Did you know that?

Beetroot was originally cultivated for its leaves. It was the ancient Greeks who firs cultivated them around 300 BC.

30

Pulisseri

Pulisseri is a simple curry that can be made in an instance using readily available ingredients from your kitchen.

Preparation time: 20 minutes

Serves: 8 guests

Ingredients

Curd: 1 kg

Water: ½ cup

Grated coconut: ½ coconut

Cumin seeds: ½ tsp

Turmeric powder: ¼ tsp

Green chillies: 2-3 nos.

Ginger: 1 small piece, grated

Garlic flakes: 2 nos. (optional)

Salt to taste

Seasoning

Mustard seeds: ½ tsp

Red chillies: 2 to 3

Whole fenugreek seeds: 8 to 10

Fenugreek roasted powder: a pinch

Red chilli powder: a pinch

Shallots: 2, finely chopped or round thin shape

Coconut oil: 3 tbsp

Curry leaves: 1 sprig

Preparation

- Beat or churn the curd to attain smooth mixture. You may add some water, but maintain a thick consistency. Keep it aside.

- Grind coconut, garlic, turmeric powder, cumin seeds, green chilies, and curry leaves (option) with 2 to 3 tablespoons of water to a fine paste.

- Now heat an earthern pot or any other pan. Add this coconut mixture and keep stirring. Bring this mixture to a boil and keep on stirring till the rawness evaporates.

- On a low flame, add the curd and give it a good mix. Add salt. Do not boil this gravy once the curd is added. Switch off the flame.

Seasoning

- Heat a seasoning pan and add 2 tablespoons of oil.

- Add mustard seeds; once they splutter, add fenugreek seeds, red chillies and chopped shallots. Once this mix turns crisp, add curry leaves, grated ginger and a dash of red chilli powder. Switch off the flame and garnish the Pulisseri with this mix.

TIPS

Using garlic is optional.

Do not boil the gravy once curd is added.

Add salt to taste.

While seasoning, take utmost care to keep on low flame and don't burn the mustard seeds/ curry leaves /red chilles etc. It will spoil the taste.

....

Did you know that?

The curd in the Pulisseri helps contains healthy bacteria to promote gut health.

Sambaram

All the colas of the world do not stand a chance in the presence of the mighty Sambaram! Refreshing, nutritious and an absolute thirst quencher.

Preparation time: 10 minutes

Serves: 6 guests

Ingredients

Fresh curd: ½ kg

Water: 1 l

Shallots: 6 to 7

Green chillies: 2 to 3 (preferably Kanthari mulagu-bird eye chillies)

Ginger: ½ inch

Curry leaves

Lemon leaves/Lemon zest: 2 to 3 pieces

Salt to taste

Preparation

- Crush the shallots, green chillies, ginger, curry leaves and salt.

- Churn the curd well with a Mattu/madhani (whipper) and add 1 litre of cold water until you attain a smooth mixture and then keep it aside.

- Add the crushed ingredients into this buttermilk and give it a very good mix.

- Check if the salt is as per your taste.

- Crush few lemon leaves on your palms and add them to this mixture.

TIPS

Lemon zest or lemon leaves are optional.

Use cold water.

Add more water or curd depending on the quantity you want to make. Increase or reduce the ingredients according to your taste.

Did you know that?

Buttermilk is a natural coolant. It also combats hot flashes in menopausal women.

34

AAHARAM | SADHYA

Paal Payasam

Milk and rice dessert- Paal Payasam is what a sadhya eater longs for. It is the crowning glory of the sadhya and if the Paal Payasam doesn't turn out right, the entire sadhya loses points.

Preparation time: 45 minutes

Serves: 10 to 12 guests

Ingredients

Rice: ¼ kg (long grain/short grain /raw rice). I use Kerala payasam rice (Unakkalari/Pacchari)

Sugar: ½ kg

Milk: 2 ½ l

Water: 1½ l

Cardamom: 4 to 5, crushed

Cashewnuts: 15 (Roasted)

Raisins: 15

Ghee: 2 to 3 tbsp (cow milk)

Tulsi leaves: 5 to 6

Rose petals: 2 to 3 (optional)

Preparation

- Wash the rice properly and soak it in water. Keep aside for half an hour before preparation.

- In an uruli (heavy-bottomed shallow vessel), add 1½ litre of water and bring this to a boil. On a medium flame, add 1½ litres of milk. Stir it well and bring this to a boil. Keep stirring continuously.

- Now, add the soaked rice and give it a good mix. Keep stirring on medium flame. Allow the milk, water, and rice to blend and cook very well.

- Once the rice is cooked well, add the remaining 1 litre of milk; keep stirring.

- Now, add sugar and keep stirring till the milk gets thicker in consistency.

- Continue stirring. Then, add two tablespoons of cow ghee. You will notice the payasam is getting ready as the colour of this mixture changes.

- Keep checking the consistency and ensure the milk doesn't get burnt. The entire process is only from low to medium and medium to low flame.

- Now is the time to add crushed cardamom, followed by 1 tablespoon of ghee and 2 to 3 leaves of tulsi/rose petals, and roasted cashewnuts. Close the uruli with a proper lid. Allow this to cool and Paal Payasam is ready to be served.

TIPS

You may use any rice of your choice as mentioned in the ingredients list.

Keep on stirring continuously on medium flame to avoid burnt smell.

Allow the mixture to be thick in consistency.

Cashewnuts/Raisins etc. are optional.

Did you know that?

The first mention of a milk and sugar dessert was found in Gujarat in the 14th century. It is linked to temples and not surprising at all, it is indeed food fit for the Gods.

Ada Pradhaman

Desserts are an intrinsic part of every sadhya. Ada Pradhaman is a much loved one. The consistency is pudding like, thereby posing a challenge to eat on the leaf sans cutlery.

Preparation time: 45 minutes

Serves: 8 to 10 guests

Ingredients

Rice ada of any brand: 200 g

Jaggery: 400 g

Sago (optional): ½ cup

Coconut milk 1st extract (thick): 2 cups

Coconut milk 2nd extract (thin): 2½ cups

Cow milk (optional) in case coconut milk is not enough

Dry ginger powder: 1 tsp

Cumin powder (optional): ½ tsp

Cardamom powder: 1½ tsp

Ghee: 6 tsp

Sliced coconut (very small pieces): ½ cup

Seasoning

Ghee: 3 tbsp

Sliced coconut

Cashewnuts: 50 g

Raisins: 50 g

Preparation

- Wash the ada very well with cold water. Strain the water and keep aside.

- Add approximately 1½ litres of water and bring to a boil. Now add the ada and allow it to cook well on a medium flame. Add 1 teaspoon of ghee. Keep stirring while cooking so that it doesn't get sticky. Once the ada is cooked well and it has achieved a soft texture, switch off the flame.

- Now, drain the water and pour cold water 2 to 3 times, strain the ada and keep it aside.

- In a vessel, add two cups of water followed by the jaggery pieces, and bring it to a boil. Once the jaggery water is boiled well without any lumps, switch off the flame. Keep the jaggery water aside.

- Strain the jaggery water using a sieve to remove the unwanted solid components before adding in the ada.

- On a medium flame, in an uruli, add 1 teaspoon of ghee, pour the jaggery water and bring it to a boil. Stir it continuously and then add the cooked ada to this jaggery syrup. It is the right time to add the cooked sago (sabudana). Stir at regular intervals and keep the flame low; jaggery will begin to thicken.

This is the important part of Ada Pradhaman.

- Add only half a cup of the first extract thick coconut milk and stir it for 3 to 4 minutes. Stir it well; on medium flame, add the full third extract of coconut milk. Let it boil well, but ensure that the ada doesn't become sticky. Now, add the full second extract of coconut milk and allow it boil.

- Check the consistency and softness of the ada while stirring, this is the right time to add the rest of the coconut milk of the first extract. But do not boil the same. Just heat it on a low flame and switch off the flame.

- Now add dry ginger powder, cardamom and cumin powder. Add 2 tablespoons of ghee and mix it well.

Seasoning

- In a frying pan, add ghee and roast cashewnuts, raisins and coconut pieces one by one; garnish the Ada Pradhaman generously.

- It is ready to be served once it cools down. You can also have it hot with banana or pappadam on a banana leaf, the traditional way.

TIPS

You may use readymade coconut milk if unable to extract coconut milk at home Just follow the process by diluting and adding at regular intervals.

We can mix cow milk as well in case coconut milk is less.

Cumin powder is optional. You can add cooked sago into the pradhaman (Optional)

Sago is optional.

Did you know that?

It is said that one should eat a piece of jaggery after every meal. It wards off constipation and aids in digestion.

Banana Chips

—

A perfect crackling accompaniment with the delicious curries, these chips are everybody's favourite.

Preparation time: 30 minutes

Serves: 50 guests

—

Ingredients

Raw banana (Ethakka): 1 kg

Turmeric powder: ½ tsp

Coconut oil: 1 litre

Salt to taste

Water: ¼ cup water to make salt water to sprinkle on the chips.

Preparation

- Peel the skin of the raw bananas and dip them in water. Drain the water off completely.

- Slice the bananas uniformly, ensuring medium thickness. You could use a slicer for chips or a regular kitchen knife.

- Mix ½ a teaspoon turmeric powder and salt in 1/4 cup of water.

- Heat oil in a frying pan (uruli). Slide the sliced bananas into it. Fry on high flame, initially, and then on medium. Do not stir until the chips start turning crispy.

- Now, sprinkle 2 to 3 teaspoons of turmeric powder and salt water into the oil.

- Once the sizzling sound settles down, remove the chips from the pan and spread them on an oil absorber sheet/ tissue paper. Remove the chips from the pan and spread them on an oil absorber sheet/ tissue paper.

- You may sprinkle salt water if you require more salt, and mix well using your hands.

- Once the chips cool down, store them in an airtight container.

TIPS

Dip the raw, peeled banana slices in salt and turmeric water for 5 to 7 minutes.

Apply coconut oil on your palms while slicing the bananas.

Health benefits

Banana chips are a source of magnesium, vitamin A, phosporous and potassium.

Chakka (jackfruit) Chips

A perfect crackling accompaniment with the delicious curries, these chips are everybody's favourite.

Preparation time: 30 minutes

Serves: 50 guests

Ingredients

Raw jackfruit: 1 kg

Turmeric powder: ½ tsp

Coconut oil: 1 litre

Salt to taste

Water: ¼ cup, to make saltwater and sprinkle on the chips

Preparation

- Peel the skin of the whole jackfruit. Remove the seeds from the fruit and keep aside.

- Slice the fruit segments into juliennes (thin, long slices).

- Mix half a teaspoon of turmeric powder and salt in 1/4 cup of water.

- In a frying pan (uruli), heat some oil. Slide the jackfruit slices into it. Fry on high flame, initially, and then keep it on medium. Do not stir until the chips start turning crispy.

- Sprinkle 2 to 3 teaspoons of turmeric and salt water into the oil. Once the bubbles or the sizzling sound settles down, remove the chips from the pan and spread them on an oil absorber sheet/tissue paper.

- Remove the chips from the pan and spread them on an oil absorber sheet/tissue paper.

- Add salt water if needed and mix well using your hands.

- Once the chips are cool, store in an airtight container.

TIPS

Jackfruit has a lot of gum. So, oil your palms before cutting.

....

Health benefits

Jackfruit is a great source of energy and is great for digestion.

42

AAHARAM | SADHYA

Sharkaravaratti Upperi

(Jaggery Chips)

—

The first thing the eye seeks out in the green leaf of the sadhya is the unmistakable brown of the sharkaravaratti next to the delightful yellow of the banana chips. The sweet crunchy banana chunks deep fried and flavoured with ginger is the stuff of childhood delights.

Preparation time: 30 minutes

Serves: 50 guests

Ingredients

Raw banana: 500 g

Jaggery: 250 g

Sugar: 1 tbsp, powdered

Dry ginger (chukku): 1 tsp

Cardamom powder: 3 to 4 cloves

Cumin powder: ½ tsp

Turmeric powder: ¼ tsp

Rice powder: 2 tsp, roasted

Salt: ½ tsp

Water: To sprinkle along with salt

Preparation

- Peel the raw banana and let it soak in salt and turmeric water for 5 to 7 minutes.

- Drain the water completely and dry the same with a clean napkin.

- Cut the bananas into long pieces.

- Heat oil in a frying pan, and then slide the cut bananas into it. Fry on medium flame until the chips start turning crispy. Set the fried banana chips aside.

- Spread them on an oil absorber sheet/tissue paper.

- Melt the jaggery in water. Strain the jaggery water and bring it to a boil in a pan on medium flame.

- This is the perfect time to add half of the spices like cardamom, cumin, dry ginger and salt. Give it a good mix.

- Now add the fried banana chips into this mixture and stir it well and keep this aside.

- This is the best time to add the other spices and some powdered sugar. Mix it well and let it dry. Add the remaining sugar and stir it well. You may add a tablespoon of rice powder, which is optional, and give it a good mix. Allow it to cool.

- Ready to serve.

TIPS

Apply coconut oil to your palms while slicing the bananas.

Matta rice

Red rice is said to be the healthiest variety of rice. It is packed with fibre and iron.

Preparation time: 45 minutes

Serves: 2 to 3 guests

Ingredients

Red rice (Matta rice): 2 cups

Water (use plenty of water to cover the rice): 10-12 cups approx.

Salt (optional)

Preparation

- Clean the rice and wash thoroughly with cold water. Soak it approximately for 45 minutes.

- Fill a wide thick bottomed vessel or earthen pot with water and bring it to a boil. When the water is sufficiently boiled, add the soaked rice and give it a good mix. It will take approximately 45 minutes to an hour for the rice to cook well.

- To check if the rice is cooked, press a few grains using your fingers.

- Once the rice is cooked well, remove the excess water using a rice draining colander.

TIPS

You may pressure cook this rice with 4 to 5 cups of water with 3 to 4 whistles.

....

Did you know that?

The red rice gets it colour from anthocyanin, anthocyanin is found in many red and purple vegetables.

Ghee

A few drops of aromatic, wholesome nutrition meets steaming rice. Magic.

Pappadam

The crisp, crackling pappadams take the deliciousness of the sadhya to another level.

Salt

Salt is in one corner of the plantain leaf, like on standby in case it's needed. Usually it's left untouched, probably the only item on the leaf that is.

On auspicious days and special occasions like birthdays, a traditional lamp is lit before serving the sadhya. The food is first offered to the Gods.

Traditionally, one should sit facing east on the floor. By sitting in this position, the digestive process is eased. The best way to relish sadhya is with your hands. This practice is believed to help fingertips connect with the heart and facilitate emotional and physical well-being.

A plantain leaf should be positioned so that it points to the left of the guests. Once the meal is finished, the leaf should be folded and closed. Closing the leaf indicates that one is satisfied with the meal.

Plantain leaves are 100% natural and hygienic. Oil and ghee do not stick to leaves. On the day of Sadhya, approximately 20 to 30 items are made (called vibhavangal), and each is served at a specific position with all dry items on the top half, and gravy items on the bottom half.

01	Salt (Uppu)	15	Mezhukkupuratti
02	Sharkaravaratti	16	Mathanga Erisseri
03	Upperi(Banana Chips)	17	Rice
04	Jackfruit Chips(Chakka)	18	Ghee(Nei)
05	Naranga Currry	19	Parippu
06	Kadugu Maanga(Mango)	20	Pappadam
07	Injipuli	21	Sambhar
08	Beetroot Pachhadi	22	Puliserry
09	pineapple Pachhadi	23	Rasam
10	Olan	24	Ada Pradhaman
11	Kalan	25	Paal Payasam
12	Kootu curry	26	Poovam Pazham
13	Aviyal	27	Sambaram
14	Thoran		

Kadugu Maanga (Mango Pickle)

Inji Puli

Naranga Curry

Pineapple Pachadi

Olan

Beetroot Pachadi

Kaalan

Kootu Curry

Thoran

Avial

Mathanga Erisseri

Mezhukkupuratti

Rasam

Sambaram

Pulissery

Sharkaravaratti

Pappadam

Poovan Pazham

Uppu (Salt)

Upperi (Banana Chips)

Parippu

Sambar

Chakka Chips

Ghee Nei

Matta Rice

Ada Pradhaman

Paal Payassam

The Team

Sugatha Menon
Editor

The thrill Sugatha Menon experienced
when she got her first assignment of writing
picture captions for a travel story on Guruvayur,
as an Editorial Assistant with Voyage, a travel
magazine of Parsiana Publications, remains
undimmed after almost 26 years of writing.
Since then she has traversed many paths, covered
almost every medium. From being a copywriter at
FCB Ulka where she wrote TV commercials for some
of the leading brands of India to working with
almost all the top publications there was.
From being the Assistant Editor, Femina, a job that
awoke her inner 'woman of substance' to being the
Lifestyle Editor of MSN.com to going back to print
with Jade, a lifestyle magazine for the south.
She thought she'd done it all until she ventured
into brand communications. She joined fashion
designer Anita Dongre as Head Content and
Communications and then moved on to join
Master chef Sanjeev Kapoor as Content Head.
Today she takes up writing projects that give
her time to smell the roses.

Rama Ramanan
Copy Editor

Rama Ramanan has been spinning stories to touch
hearts and her bank balance for seventeen years.
She works as Associate Editor with The New Indian
Express and heads the City Express supplement for
the Chennai edition. Less of a chatterbox, more of
a listener, she loves offering a keen ear to stories
that surround her.

She sees her vocation as a means of self-actualisation
and a path to touch the lives of readers, positively.
But when she's not writing or editing, she's scouting
for workout videos, healthy recipes, Bollywood cringe,
and being a spiritual gangsta — for a mindful and
mindless balance of life.

Vikas Swades Sharma
Commercial & Advertising Photographer

A Mumbai-based photographer and the founder of THE COLLECTIVE DEPOT, Vikas has an innate desire to learn about different people and cultures.

Respected and recognised for his unique and multidisciplinary approach to his craft. His work is bold and imaginative, creatively bringing together the demands of commercial photography.

He loves the collaborative process of creating great work. He works alongside with industry's top talents, art directors, advertising agencies, stylists and production houses as well as work directly with clients and develop something new that he hasn't created before. He covers a wide range across categories and produces over-the-top and most precise photography and films.

Radhika Tipnis
Creative Director, Visual Concept Design, Typography

Radhika studied Applied Art at undergraduate level before obtaining a Master's degree in Visual Communication at IDC, IIT Bombay. She worked in the fields of multimedia, e-learning and graphic design in Mumbai, Singapore and Hong Kong.

Her years raising twins brought her into close contact with the fascinating world of picture books, triggering a long-dormant desire to write, illustrate and design for children. Her picture books are published in English, Hindi, Marathi and Konkani. In 2019, 'Maharashtra Sahitya Parishad' awarded her books for 'Best Design and Illustration'. She curently works as a freelance visual designer and illustrator.

Nikita Rao
Art Director, Food Stylist

Backwaters Chechi's Sambhar Podi (BWC Sambhar Podi)

The spices in sambhar varies in every household. Hence, no two sambhars will ever taste the same. Here's something that's from your Backwaters Chechi. Make it and store it as well for future use.

Prep Time: 30 mins

Ingredients

Kashmiri chilli: 50 g

Normal red chilli: 50 g

Coriander seeds: 50 g

Fenugreek seeds: 2 tbsp

Chana dal: 3 tbsp

Urad dal: 2 tbsp

Tur dal: 1 tbsp

Curry leaves: 2 to 3 sprigs

Turmeric powder: 1 tsp

Asafoetida: 1 tsp

Preparation

- The cooking time for each ingredient is different. Hence, dry roast each ingredient from numbers 1 to 11 separately, in batches, on a low flame and keep it aside on a plate.

- Remember to sauté the coriander seeds until they turn crunchy. Deep-roast the fenugreek seeds.

- The curry leaves should be roasted until they turn crisp. Roast the whole turmeric or turmeric powder, at the end.

- Mix all of them and grind to a smooth powder.

- You can add more of fenugreek or asafoetida as per your taste.

- Turmeric is added as a preservative.

- If you are making in a large quantity, add 1 teaspoon of castor oil to maintain the moisture.

Tip: You may add one teaspoon of cumin seeds /pepper 1 tsp if you like. In authentic Kerala Sambhar, we do not use cumin seeds as it changes the authentic taste.

Any type of rice can be used.

www.ingramcontent.com/pod-product-compliance
Lightning Source LLC
Chambersburg PA
CBHW040453100426

42813CB00022BA/2990